MY 90 DAYS

DIET
JOURNAL

ISBN-13: 978-1541338777
ISBN-10: 1541338774

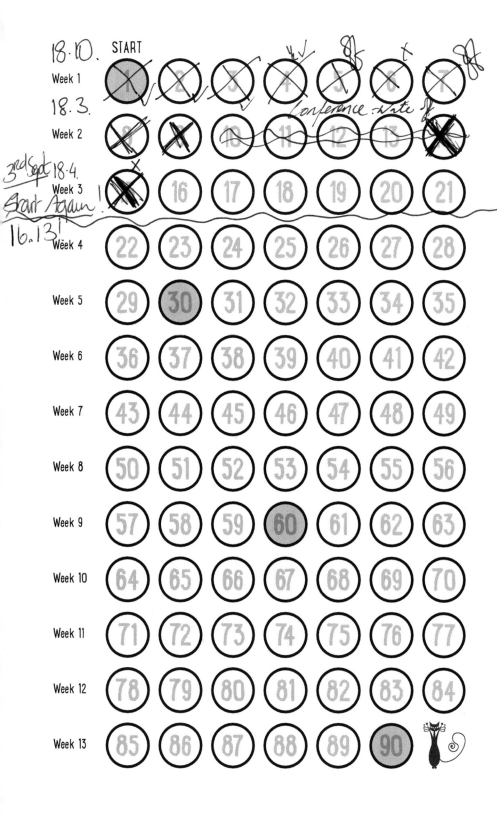

Sept. Day 30th

 Day ① **START**

My Measurements

Arm
16 R
15¾ L

Hips
54½
around hip bone

Calf
18 R
18 L

Chest 48½
Waist 45
Belly 49
Between Butt +
navel
Thigh 34 R
33 L

Weight ....
BMI ....

My Goals ....
....
....
....
....
....

Day ①

Breakfast	Lunch	Dinner
....	....	....
....	....	....
....	....	....
....	....	....
....	....	....
Snacks	....	....
....	....	....
....	....	....
....	....	....
....	....	....

6a 7 8 9 10 11 12p 1 2 3 4 5 6 7 8 9 10+

B=Breakfast L=Lunch D=Dinner S=Snack E=Exercise M=Mind

Exercise ....

Mind ....

Emotional State

Contentment

0%   50%   100%

Sleep   Sleeping Time ....   # Times Wake Up at Night ....

Notes   ....

....

....

....

....

Date .... Mo Tu We Th Fr Sa Su

Day ②

Breakfast
....
....
....
....
....

Snacks
....
....
....
....

Lunch
....
....
....
....
....
....
....
....
....
....

Dinner
....
....
....
....
....
....
....
....
....
....

🕐 6a 7 8 9 10 11 12p 1 2 3 4 5 6 7 8 9 10+
B=Breakfast L=Lunch D=Dinner S=Snack E=Exercise M=Mind

Exercise ....

Mind ....

Emotional State
😀 ◯   🙂 ◯   😐 ◯   🙁 ◯

Contentment
0%   50%   100%

Sleep   Sleeping Time ....   # Times Wake Up at Night ....

Notes
....
....
....
....
....

Day ③

Date .... Mo Tu We Th Fr Sa Su

Breakfast	Lunch	Dinner
....	....	....
....	....	....
....	....	....
....	....	....
....	....	....
Snacks	....	....
....	....	....
....	....	....
....	....	....
....	....	....

6a 7 8 9 10 11 12p 1 2 3 4 5 6 7 8 9 10+

B=Breakfast L=Lunch D=Dinner S=Snack E=Exercise M=Mind

Exercise ....

Mind ....

Emotional State   **Contentment**

○ ○ ○ ○   0%   50%   100%

Sleep   Sleeping Time ....   # Times Wake Up at Night ....

Notes ....
....
....
....
....

Date 25/1/2018   Mo Tu We (Th) Fr Sa Su   Day (4)

Breakfast
Porridge

fasting Bloods
so late
brekkie

Snacks

Lunch
1 Bar

Dinner
Coke
Snack
Crisps

| 6a | 7 | 8 | 9 | 10 | B | 11 | 12p | 1 | 2 | 3 | 4 | 5 | 6 | 7 | 8 | 9 | 10+ |

B=Breakfast L=Lunch D=Dinner S=Snack E=Exercise M=Mind

Exercise

Mind Good

Emotional State

Contentment

0%   50%   100%

Sleep 9   **Sleeping Time**   **# Times Wake Up at Night** Excellent

Notes

Day (5)

Date 26/1/2018   Mo Tu We Th (Fr) Sa Su

Breakfast
Up at 1
2 litres drank

Lunch
Porridge

Dinner
Fork @ Cinema +
1 l Water.

Steamed Scallops
— Garlic on the side.

Snacks
Crisps
1 can cola

6a 7 8 9 10 11 12p (1) 2 3 4 5 (6) 7 (8) 9 10+

B=Breakfast L=Lunch D=Dinner S=Snack E=Exercise M=Mind

Exercise

Mind   Tired am, Good

Emotional State

Contentment

0%   50%   100%

Sleep   Sleeping Time ....   # Times Wake Up at Night ....

Notes

Date 27/1/2018   Mo Tu We Th Fr (Sa) Su   Day (6)

Breakfast
Porridge.

Lunch
Ber.

Dinner
Crisps
Wafer
3 n Jellys

Snacks

6a	7	8	9	10	11	12p	1	2	3	4	5	6	7	8	9	10+

B=Breakfast L=Lunch D=Dinner S=Snack E=Exercise M=Mind

Exercise

Mind Good.

Emotional State

Contentment

0%   50%   100%

Sleep   Sleeping Time ....   # Times Wake Up at Night ....

00447 867 512 744

Notes

Day (7)

Date 28/1/2018   Mo Tu We Th Fr Sa (Su)

Breakfast
Porridge (150)

Lunch
Drumstick (100)
1 pc popcorn.
tf
KFC.

Dinner
Wafer (200)
Crisps (100)

Snacks

6a 7 8 9 10 11 12p 1 2 3 4 5 6 7 8 9 10+

B=Breakfast L=Lunch D=Dinner S=Snack E=Exercise M=Mind

Exercise

Mind

Emotional State   **Contentment**

0%   50%   100%

Sleep   Sleeping Time ....   # Times Wake Up at Night ....

Notes   Pharmaton ✓

Date 29/1/2018. (Mo) Tu We Th Fr Sa Su   Day (8)

Breakfast
Porridge.

Lunch
Berl

Dinner
Omlette
Chilli

Wafer.
Crisps.

Snacks
Drainer

6a 7 8 9 10 11 12p 1 2 3 4 5 6 7 8 9 10+

B=Breakfast L=Lunch D=Dinner S=Snack E=Exercise M=Mind

Exercise

Mind

Emotional State

Contentment

0%   50%   100%

Sleep   Sleeping Time ....   # Times Wake Up at Night ....

Notes

Day (9)

600

Breakfast

Porridge (150)

Lunch

Crisps (100)
Bar (150)

Dinner

5 lamb
chops
2 Poppadoms.

Snacks

Rainer.
Wafer (20)

	6a	7	8	9	10	11	12p	1	2	3	4	5	6	7	8	9	10+

B=Breakfast   L=Lunch   D=Dinner   S=Snack   E=Exercise   M=Mind

Exercise ....

Mind ....

Emotional State

⊙ ☺ ☺ ☹
○ ○ ○ ○

Contentment

0%   50%   100%

Sleep   Sleeping Time ....   # Times Wake Up at Night ....

Notes ....
....
....
....
....

Date _5/2/2018._ (Mo) Tu We Th Fr Sa Su   Day (10)

Breakfast	Lunch	Dinner

Snacks
2 Wafers.
3 Crisps
1 Bar.

6a 7 8 9 10 11 12p 1 2 3 4 5 6 7 8 9 10+

B=Breakfast L=Lunch D=Dinner S=Snack E=Exercise M=Mind

Exercise ....

Mind .... Tired ....

Emotional State   **Contentment**

0%   50%   100%

Sleep   Sleeping Time ....   # Times Wake Up at Night ....

Notes

Day (11)

Date .... Mo Tu We Th Fr Sa Su

Breakfast

....
....
....
....
....

Snacks

....
....
....
....

Lunch

....
....
....
....
....
....
....
....
....

Dinner

....
....
....
....
....
....
....
....
....

6a 7 8 9 10 11 12p 1 2 3 4 5 6 7 8 9 10+

B=Breakfast L=Lunch D=Dinner S=Snack E=Exercise M=Mind

Exercise ....

Mind ....

Emotional State

○ ○ ○ ○

Contentment

0%   50%   100%

Sleep   Sleeping Time ....   # Times Wake Up at Night ....

Notes

....
....
....
....
....

Date .... Mo Tu We Th Fr Sa Su

Day (12)

Breakfast	Lunch	Dinner
....	....	....
....	....	....
....	....	....
....	....	....
....	....	....
Snacks	....	....
....	....	....
....	....	....
....	....	....
....	....	....

6a 7 8 9 10 11 12p 1 2 3 4 5 6 7 8 9 10+

B=Breakfast L=Lunch D=Dinner S=Snack E=Exercise M=Mind

Exercise ....

Mind ....

Emotional State

😀 🙂 😐 🙁
○ ○ ○ ○

Contentment

0%   50%   100%

Sleep   Sleeping Time ....   # Times Wake Up at Night ....

....

....

....

Notes

....

....

Day (13)

Date .... Mo Tu We Th Fr Sa Su

Breakfast

....
....
....
....
....

Snacks

....
....
....
....

Lunch

....
....
....
....
....
....
....
....
....

Dinner

....
....
....
....
....

🕐 6a 7 8 9 10 11 12p 1 2 3 4 5 6 7 8 9 10+

B=Breakfast L=Lunch D=Dinner S=Snack E=Exercise M=Mind

Exercise ....

Mind ....

Emotional State   **Contentment**

😄 😊 😐 ☹️

○ ○ ○ ○   0%   50%   100%

Sleep   Sleeping Time ....   # Times Wake Up at Night ....

Notes

....
....
....
....
....

Date .... Mo Tu We Th Fr Sa Su

Breakfast	Lunch	Dinner
....	....	....
....	....	....
....	....	....
....	....	....
....	....	....
Snacks	....	....
....	....	....
....	....	....
....	....	....
....	....	....

| 6a | 7 | 8 | 9 | 10 | 11 | 12p | 1 | 2 | 3 | 4 | 5 | 6 | 7 | 8 | 9 | 10+ |

B=Breakfast L=Lunch D=Dinner S=Snack E=Exercise M=Mind

Exercise ....

Mind ....

Emotional State

○ ○ ○ ○

Contentment

0%   50%   100%

Sleep   Sleeping Time ....   # Times Wake Up at Night ....

....   **Notes**

....

....

....

....

Day

Date ....   Mo Tu We Th Fr Sa Su

Breakfast	Lunch	Dinner
....	....	....
....	....	....
....	....	....
....	....	....
....	....	....
Snacks	....	....
....	....	....
....	....	....
....	....	....
....	....	....

6a 7 8 9 10 11 12p 1 2 3 4 5 6 7 8 9 10+

B=Breakfast L=Lunch D=Dinner S=Snack E=Exercise M=Mind

Exercise ....

Mind ....

Emotional State

😁 ☺ 😐 ☹
○ ○ ○ ○

Contentment

0%   50%   100%

Sleep   Sleeping Time ....   # Times Wake Up at Night ....

Notes   ....
....
....
....

Date ....   Mo Tu We Th Fr Sa Su

Breakfast	Lunch	Dinner
....	....	....
....	....	....
....	....	....
....	....	....
....	....	....
	....	....
Snacks	....	....
....	....	....
....	....	....
....	....	....
....	....	....

🕐   6a   7   8   9   10   11   12p   1   2   3   4   5   6   7   8   9   10+
....
B=Breakfast   L=Lunch   D=Dinner   S=Snack   E=Exercise   M=Mind

Exercise ....

Mind ....

Emotional State

😃 🙂 😐 🙁
○   ○   ○   ○

Contentment

0%   50%   100%

Sleep   Sleeping Time ....   # Times Wake Up at Night ....

....

....   Notes

....

....

....

Day (17)

Date .... Mo Tu We Th Fr Sa Su

Breakfast

....
....
....
....
....

Snacks

....
....
....
....

Lunch

....
....
....
....
....
....
....
....
....
....

Dinner

....
....
....
....
....
....
....
....
....
....

6a 7 8 9 10 11 12p 1 2 3 4 5 6 7 8 9 10+

B=Breakfast L=Lunch D=Dinner S=Snack E=Exercise M=Mind

Exercise ....

Mind ....

Emotional State

○ ○ ○ ○

Contentment

0%   50%   100%

Sleep   Sleeping Time ....   # Times Wake Up at Night ....

Notes

....
....
....
....
....

Date ....   Mo Tu We Th Fr Sa Su   Day (18)

Breakfast	Lunch	Dinner
....	....	....
....	....	....
....	....	....
....	....	....
....	....	....
Snacks	....	....
....	....	....
....	....	....
....	....	....
....	....	....

🕐 6a 7 8 9 10 11 12p 1 2 3 4 5 6 7 8 9 10+

B=Breakfast L=Lunch D=Dinner S=Snack E=Exercise M=Mind

Exercise ....

Mind ....

Emotional State   **Contentment**

😀 🙂 😐 🙁

○   ○   ○   ○   0%   50%   100%

Sleep   Sleeping Time ....   # Times Wake Up at Night ....

....   **Notes**

....

....

....

....

Day 19

Date ....   Mo Tu We Th Fr Sa Su

Breakfast	Lunch	Dinner
....	....	....
....	....	....
....	....	....
....	....	....
....	....	....
Snacks	....	....
....	....	....
....	....	....
....	....	....
....		

6a   7   8   9   10   11   12p   1   2   3   4   5   6   7   8   9   10+

B=Breakfast   L=Lunch   D=Dinner   S=Snack   E=Exercise   M=Mind

Exercise ....

Mind ....

Emotional State
😃 🙂 😐 ☹️
○   ○   ○   ○

Contentment
0%   50%   100%

Sleep   Sleeping Time ....   # Times Wake Up at Night ....

Notes ....
....
....
....
....

Date .... Mo Tu We Th Fr Sa Su

Breakfast	Lunch	Dinner
....	....	....
....	....	....
....	....	....
....	....	....
....	....	....
Snacks	....	....
....	....	....
....	....	....
....	....	....
....	....	....

🕐 6a 7 8 9 10 11 12p 1 2 3 4 5 6 7 8 9 10+

B=Breakfast L=Lunch D=Dinner S=Snack E=Exercise M=Mind

Exercise ....

Mind ....

Emotional State

😀 ○   🙂 ○   😐 ○   🙁 ○

Contentment

0%   50%   100%

Sleep   Sleeping Time ....   # Times Wake Up at Night ....

....

....

....

....

....

Notes

Day (21)

Date .... Mo Tu We Th Fr Sa Su

Breakfast
....
....
....
....
....

Snacks
....
....
....
....

Lunch
....
....
....
....
....
....
....
....
....
....
....
....

Dinner
....
....
....
....
....
....

6a 7 8 9 10 11 12p 1 2 3 4 5 6 7 8 9 10+

B=Breakfast L=Lunch D=Dinner S=Snack E=Exercise M=Mind

Exercise ....

Mind ....

Emotional State

○ ○ ○ ○

Contentment

0%   50%   100%

Sleep   Sleeping Time ....   # Times Wake Up at Night ....

Notes   ....
....
....
....
....

Date ....   Mo Tu We Th Fr Sa Su

Breakfast	Lunch	Dinner
....	....	....
....	....	....
....	....	....
....	....	....
....	....	....
Snacks	....	....
....	....	....
....	....	....
....	....	....
....	....	....

6a   7   8   9   10   11   12p   1   2   3   4   5   6   7   8   9   10+

B=Breakfast   L=Lunch   D=Dinner   S=Snack   E=Exercise   M=Mind

Exercise ....

Mind ....

Emotional State

Contentment

0%   50%   100%

Sleep   Sleeping Time ....   # Times Wake Up at Night ....

....

....   **Notes**

....

....

....

Day (23)

Breakfast	Lunch	Dinner
....	....	....
....	....	....
....	....	....
....	....	....
....	....	....
Snacks	....	....
....	....	....
....	....	....
....	....	....
....		....

6a 7 8 9 10 11 12p 1 2 3 4 5 6 7 8 9 10+

B=Breakfast L=Lunch D=Dinner S=Snack E=Exercise M=Mind

Exercise ....

Mind ....

Emotional State

Contentment

0%   50%   100%

Sleep   Sleeping Time ....   # Times Wake Up at Night ....

Notes ....
....
....
....
....

Date ....   Mo Tu We Th Fr Sa Su   Day (24)

Breakfast

....
....
....
....
....

Snacks

....
....
....
....

Lunch

....
....
....
....
....
....
....
....
....
....
....
....
....

Dinner

....
....
....
....
....
....
....
....
....
....
....
....

| 6a | 7 | 8 | 9 | 10 | 11 | 12p | 1 | 2 | 3 | 4 | 5 | 6 | 7 | 8 | 9 | 10+ |

B=Breakfast   L=Lunch   D=Dinner   S=Snack   E=Exercise   M=Mind

Exercise ....

Mind ....

Emotional State

😃 ⌣ ☺ 😐 ☹
○   ○   ○   ○

Contentment

0%   50%   100%

Sleep   Sleeping Time ....   # Times Wake Up at Night ....

Notes

....
....
....
....
....

Day (25)

Date .... Mo Tu We Th Fr Sa Su

Breakfast

....

....

....

....

....

Snacks

....

....

....

....

Lunch

....

....

....

....

....

....

....

....

....

....

Dinner

....

....

....

....

....

....

....

....

....

....

| 6a | 7 | 8 | 9 | 10 | 11 | 12p | 1 | 2 | 3 | 4 | 5 | 6 | 7 | 8 | 9 | 10+ |

B=Breakfast L=Lunch D=Dinner S=Snack E=Exercise M=Mind

Exercise ....

Mind ....

Emotional State

☺ ☺ ☺ ☹
○ ○ ○ ○

Contentment

0%   50%   100%

Sleep   Sleeping Time ....   # Times Wake Up at Night ....

Notes   ....

....

....

....

....

Date .... Mo Tu We Th Fr Sa Su   Day (26)

Breakfast	Lunch	Dinner
....	....	....
....	....	....
....	....	....
....	....	....
....	....	....
Snacks	....	....
....	....	....
....	....	....
....	....	....
....	....	....

🕐 6a 7 8 9 10 11 12p 1 2 3 4 5 6 7 8 9 10+

B=Breakfast L=Lunch D=Dinner S=Snack E=Exercise M=Mind

Exercise ....

Mind ....

Emotional State   ### Contentment

😀 🙂 😐 🙁

0%   50%   100%

Sleep   Sleeping Time ....   # Times Wake Up at Night ....

....   **Notes**

....

....

....

....

Day 27

Date .... Mo Tu We Th Fr Sa Su

Breakfast

....
....
....
....
....

Snacks

....
....
....
....

Lunch

....
....
....
....
....
....
....
....
....
....

Dinner

....
....
....
....
....

6a 7 8 9 10 11 12p 1 2 3 4 5 6 7 8 9 10+
B=Breakfast L=Lunch D=Dinner S=Snack E=Exercise M=Mind

Exercise ....

Mind ....

Emotional State

○ ○ ○ ○

Contentment

0%   50%   100%

Sleep   Sleeping Time ....   # Times Wake Up at Night ....

Notes ....
....
....
....
....

Date .... Mo Tu We Th Fr Sa Su   Day (28)

Breakfast	Lunch	Dinner
....	....	....
....	....	....
....	....	....
....	....	....
....	....	....
Snacks	....	....
....	....	....
....	....	....
....	....	....
....	....	....

🕐   6a   7   8   9   10   11   12p   1   2   3   4   5   6   7   8   9   10+

B=Breakfast   L=Lunch   D=Dinner   S=Snack   E=Exercise   M=Mind

Exercise ....

Mind ....

Emotional State   Contentment

😀 🙂 😐 🙁   0%   50%   100%

○   ○   ○   ○

Sleep   Sleeping Time ....   # Times Wake Up at Night ....

....   Notes

....

....

....

....

Day (29)

Date .... Mo Tu We Th Fr Sa Su

Breakfast	Lunch	Dinner
....	....	....
....	....	....
....	....	....
....	....	....
....	....	....
Snacks	....	
....	....	
....	....	
....	....	
....	....	

6a 7 8 9 10 11 12p 1 2 3 4 5 6 7 8 9 10+
....

B=Breakfast L=Lunch D=Dinner S=Snack E=Exercise M=Mind

Exercise ....

Mind ....

Emotional State

○ ○ ○ ○

Contentment

0%   50%   100%

Sleep   Sleeping Time ....   # Times Wake Up at Night ....

Notes   ....
....
....
....
....

12ᵀᴴ Sept 2019

Day (30) **BREAKPOINT**

My Measurements

Oct - R - 14¼
    L - 14½
    R 14½
Arm∠ 14¾

Oct - 51
Hips 51½

Oct - R = 17¾
   ∠ 17¼
     R - 18¼
Calf 1 - 17¾

14ᵀᴴ Oct 2019
↓
25½   Chest 46½
40½   Waist 40½
48   Belly 51
Between Button +
Knicker line
         Thigh
R - 30½ - Oct
            30½
∠ - 30   30

Weight   16·6·8
BMI   39·9
Oct - 16·7·
      39·7·

Oct
Notes   - 1
      - 3
      ½
      ½
      1
     6 inches

Day (30)

Date ....   Mo Tu We Th Fr Sa Su

Breakfast

....
....
....
....
....

Snacks

....
....
....
....

Lunch

....
....
....
....
....
....
....
....
....
....

Dinner

....
....
....
....
....

| 6a | 7 | 8 | 9 | 10 | 11 | 12p | 1 | 2 | 3 | 4 | 5 | 6 | 7 | 8 | 9 | 10+ |

B=Breakfast L=Lunch D=Dinner S=Snack E=Exercise M=Mind

Exercise ....

Mind ....

Emotional State

○ ○ ○ ○

Contentment

0%   50%   100%

Sleep   Sleeping Time ....   # Times Wake Up at Night ....

Notes
....
....
....
....
....

Date .... Mo Tu We Th Fr Sa Su

Day (31)

Breakfast	Lunch	Dinner
....	....	....
....	....	....
....	....	....
....	....	....
....	....	....
Snacks	....	....
....	....	....
....	....	....
....	....	....
....	....	....

| 6a | 7 | 8 | 9 | 10 | 11 | 12p | 1 | 2 | 3 | 4 | 5 | 6 | 7 | 8 | 9 | 10+ |

B=Breakfast   L=Lunch   D=Dinner   S=Snack   E=Exercise   M=Mind

Exercise ....

Mind ....

Emotional State

😀 ◯   🙂 ◯   😐 ◯   ☹️ ◯

Contentment

0%   50%   100%

Sleep   Sleeping Time ....   # Times Wake Up at Night ....

....

....

....

....

....

Notes

Day (32)

Date .... Mo Tu We Th Fr Sa Su

Breakfast	Lunch	Dinner
....	....	....
....	....	....
....	....	....
....	....	....
....	....	....
Snacks	....	....
....	....	....
....	....	....
....	....	....
....	....	....

🕐   6a   7   8   9   10   11   12p   1   2   3   4   5   6   7   8   9   10+
B=Breakfast L=Lunch D=Dinner S=Snack E=Exercise M=Mind

Exercise ....

Mind ....

Emotional State

😄 ○ 🙂 ○ 😐 ○ ☹ ○

Contentment

0%   50%   100%

Sleep   Sleeping Time ....   # Times Wake Up at Night ....

Notes   ....
....
....
....
....

Date .... Mo Tu We Th Fr Sa Su

Breakfast	Lunch	Dinner
....	....	....
....	....	....
....	....	....
....	....	....
....	....	....
	....	....
Snacks	....	....
....	....	....
....	....	....
....	....	....
....	....	....

🕐 6a 7 8 9 10 11 12p 1 2 3 4 5 6 7 8 9 10+
....
B=Breakfast L=Lunch D=Dinner S=Snack E=Exercise M=Mind

Exercise ....

Mind ....

Emotional State

😃 🙂 😐 🙁
○ ○ ○ ○

Contentment

0%   50%   100%

Sleep   Sleeping Time ....   # Times Wake Up at Night ....

....   **Notes**
....
....
....
....

Day (34)

Date .... Mo Tu We Th Fr Sa Su

Breakfast

....
....
....
....
....

Snacks

....
....
....
....

Lunch

....
....
....
....
....
....
....
....
....
....

Dinner

....
....
....
....
....
....
....
....
....
....

| 6a | 7 | 8 | 9 | 10 | 11 | 12p | 1 | 2 | 3 | 4 | 5 | 6 | 7 | 8 | 9 | 10+ |

B=Breakfast L=Lunch D=Dinner S=Snack E=Exercise M=Mind

Exercise ....

Mind ....

Emotional State

○ ○ ○ ○

Contentment

0%   50%   100%

Sleep   Sleeping Time ....   # Times Wake Up at Night ....

Notes

....
....
....
....
....

Date .... Mo Tu We Th Fr Sa Su   Day (35)

Breakfast	Lunch	Dinner
....	....	....
....	....	....
....	....	....
....	....	....
....	....	....
Snacks	....	....
....	....	....
....	....	....
....	....	....
....	....	....

6a 7 8 9 10 11 12p 1 2 3 4 5 6 7 8 9 10+

B=Breakfast L=Lunch D=Dinner S=Snack E=Exercise M=Mind

Exercise ....

Mind ....

Emotional State

Contentment

0%   50%   100%

Sleep   Sleeping Time ....   # Times Wake Up at Night ....

....

....   Notes

....

....

....

....

Day (36)

Date .... Mo Tu We Th Fr Sa Su

Breakfast	Lunch	Dinner
....	....	....
....	....	....
....	....	....
....	....	....
....	....	....
Snacks	....	
....	....	
....	....	
....	....	
....	....	

🕐 6a 7 8 9 10 11 12p 1 2 3 4 5 6 7 8 9 10+

B=Breakfast L=Lunch D=Dinner S=Snack E=Exercise M=Mind

Exercise ....

Mind ....

Emotional State

😀 ○ 🙂 ○ 😐 ○ 🙁 ○

Contentment

0%   50%   100%

Sleep Sleeping Time .... # Times Wake Up at Night ....

Notes
....
....
....
....
....

Date ....   Mo Tu We Th Fr Sa Su

Day (37)

Breakfast	Lunch	Dinner
....	....	....
....	....	....
....	....	....
....	....	....
....	....	....
Snacks	....	....
....	....	....
....	....	....
....	....	....
....	....	....

6a 7 8 9 10 11 12p 1 2 3 4 5 6 7 8 9 10+
....
B=Breakfast   L=Lunch   D=Dinner   S=Snack   E=Exercise   M=Mind

Exercise ....

Mind ....

Emotional State

😀   🙂   😐   🙁
○   ○   ○   ○

Contentment

0%   50%   100%

Sleep   Sleeping Time ....   # Times Wake Up at Night ....

....   **Notes**
....
....
....
....

Day (38)

Date .... Mo Tu We Th Fr Sa Su

Breakfast	Lunch	Dinner
....	....	....
....	....	....
....	....	....
....	....	....
....	....	....
Snacks	....	....
....	....	....
....	....	....
....	....	....
....	....	....

6a 7 8 9 10 11 12p 1 2 3 4 5 6 7 8 9 10+

B=Breakfast L=Lunch D=Dinner S=Snack E=Exercise M=Mind

Exercise ....

Mind ....

Emotional State

😀 ○ 🙂 ○ 😐 ○ 🙁 ○

Contentment

0%   50%   100%

Sleep   Sleeping Time ....   # Times Wake Up at Night ....

Notes ....
....
....
....
....

Date .... Mo Tu We Th Fr Sa Su

Day (39)

Breakfast	Lunch	Dinner
....	....	....
....	....	....
....	....	....
....	....	....
....	....	....
Snacks	....	....
....	....	....
....	....	....
....	....	....
....	....	....

6a 7 8 9 10 11 12p 1 2 3 4 5 6 7 8 9 10+

B=Breakfast L=Lunch D=Dinner S=Snack E=Exercise M=Mind

Exercise ....

Mind ....

Emotional State

Contentment

0%   50%   100%

Sleep   Sleeping Time ....   # Times Wake Up at Night ....

Notes

Day (40)

Breakfast	Lunch	Dinner
....	....	....
....	....	....
....	....	....
....	....	....
....	....	....
Snacks	....	....
....	....	....
....	....	....
....	....	....
....	....	....

🕐 6a 7 8 9 10 11 12p 1 2 3 4 5 6 7 8 9 10+

B=Breakfast L=Lunch D=Dinner S=Snack E=Exercise M=Mind

Exercise ....

Mind ....

Emotional State

☺ ☺ ☹ ☹
○ ○ ○ ○

Contentment

0%   50%   100%

Sleep   Sleeping Time ....   # Times Wake Up at Night ....

Notes   ....
....
....
....

Date ....   Mo Tu We Th Fr Sa Su   Day (41)

Breakfast	Lunch	Dinner
....	....	....
....	....	....
....	....	....
....	....	....
....	....	....
Snacks	....	....
....	....	....
....	....	....
....	....	....
....	....	....

6a 7 8 9 10 11 12p 1 2 3 4 5 6 7 8 9 10+

B=Breakfast   L=Lunch   D=Dinner   S=Snack   E=Exercise   M=Mind

Exercise ....

Mind ....

Emotional State

😀 ☺ 😐 ☹
○ ○ ○ ○

Contentment

0%   50%   100%

Sleep   Sleeping Time ....   # Times Wake Up at Night ....

Notes

....
....
....
....
....

Day (42)

Date .... Mo Tu We Th Fr Sa Su

Breakfast

....
....
....
....
....

Snacks

....
....
....
....

Lunch

....
....
....
....
....
....
....
....
....

Dinner

....
....
....
....
....
....
....
....

6a 7 8 9 10 11 12p 1 2 3 4 5 6 7 8 9 10+

B=Breakfast L=Lunch D=Dinner S=Snack E=Exercise M=Mind

Exercise ....

Mind ....

Emotional State

Contentment

0%   50%   100%

Sleep   Sleeping Time ....   **# Times Wake Up at Night** ....

Notes

....
....
....
....
....

Date .... Mo Tu We Th Fr Sa Su

Day **43**

Breakfast	Lunch	Dinner
....	....	....
....	....	....
....	....	....
....	....	....
....	....	....
Snacks	....	....
....	....	....
....	....	....
....	....	....
....	....	....

6a 7 8 9 10 11 12p 1 2 3 4 5 6 7 8 9 10+

B=Breakfast   L=Lunch   D=Dinner   S=Snack   E=Exercise   M=Mind

Exercise ....

Mind ....

Emotional State

○ ○ ○ ○

Contentment

0%   50%   100%

Sleep   Sleeping Time ....   # Times Wake Up at Night ....

....   **Notes**

....

....

....

....

Day (44)

Date .... Mo Tu We Th Fr Sa Su

Breakfast	Lunch	Dinner
....	....	....
....	....	....
....	....	....
....	....	....
....	....	....
Snacks	....	
....	....	
....	....	
....	....	
....	....	

🕐 6a 7 8 9 10 11 12p 1 2 3 4 5 6 7 8 9 10+

B=Breakfast L=Lunch D=Dinner S=Snack E=Exercise M=Mind

Exercise ....

Mind ....

Emotional State

😀 ○   🙂 ○   😐 ○   🙁 ○

Contentment

0%   50%   100%

Sleep   Sleeping Time ....   # Times Wake Up at Night ....

Notes ....

....

....

....

....

Date .... Mo Tu We Th Fr Sa Su

Breakfast	Lunch	Dinner
....	....	....
....	....	....
....	....	....
....	....	....
....	....	....
Snacks	....	....
....	....	....
....	....	....
....	....	....

6a 7 8 9 10 11 12p 1 2 3 4 5 6 7 8 9 10+

B=Breakfast L=Lunch D=Dinner S=Snack E=Exercise M=Mind

Exercise ....

Mind ....

Emotional State   Contentment

0%   50%   100%

Sleep   Sleeping Time ....   # Times Wake Up at Night ....

Notes

Day (46)

Date .... Mo Tu We Th Fr Sa Su

Breakfast
....
....
....
....
....

Snacks
....
....
....
....

Lunch
....
....
....
....
....
....
....
....
....

Dinner
....
....
....
....
....

| 6a | 7 | 8 | 9 | 10 | 11 | 12p | 1 | 2 | 3 | 4 | 5 | 6 | 7 | 8 | 9 | 10+ |

B=Breakfast L=Lunch D=Dinner S=Snack E=Exercise M=Mind

Exercise ....

Mind ....

Emotional State

😀 ☺ 😐 ☹
○   ○   ○   ○

Contentment

0%   50%   100%

Sleep   Sleeping Time ....   # Times Wake Up at Night ....

Notes
....
....
....
....
....

Date .... Mo Tu We Th Fr Sa Su

Day 47

Breakfast

....
....
....
....
....

Snacks

....
....
....
....

Lunch

....
....
....
....
....
....
....
....
....
....

Dinner

....
....
....
....
....
....
....
....
....
....

6a 7 8 9 10 11 12p 1 2 3 4 5 6 7 8 9 10+

B=Breakfast L=Lunch D=Dinner S=Snack E=Exercise M=Mind

Exercise ....

Mind ....

Emotional State

Contentment

0%   50%   100%

Sleep   Sleeping Time ....   # Times Wake Up at Night ....

....
....
....
....
....

Notes

Day (48)

Date .... Mo Tu We Th Fr Sa Su

Breakfast

....
....
....
....
....

Snacks

....
....
....
....

Lunch

....
....
....
....
....
....
....
....
....
....
....

Dinner

....
....
....
....
....
....
....
....
....
....

6a 7 8 9 10 11 12p 1 2 3 4 5 6 7 8 9 10+

B=Breakfast L=Lunch D=Dinner S=Snack E=Exercise M=Mind

Exercise ....

Mind ....

Emotional State

○ ○ ○ ○

Contentment

0%   50%   100%

Sleep   Sleeping Time ....   # Times Wake Up at Night ....

Notes
....
....
....
....
....

Date .... Mo Tu We Th Fr Sa Su

Day (49)

Breakfast	Lunch	Dinner
....	....	....
....	....	....
....	....	....
....	....	....
....	....	....
Snacks	....	....
....	....	....
....	....	....
....	....	....
....	....	....

6a 7 8 9 10 11 12p 1 2 3 4 5 6 7 8 9 10+

B=Breakfast L=Lunch D=Dinner S=Snack E=Exercise M=Mind

Exercise ....

Mind ....

Emotional State   Contentment

0%   50%   100%

Sleep   Sleeping Time ....   # Times Wake Up at Night ....

....   Notes

....

....

....

....

Day

Date ....   Mo Tu We Th Fr Sa Su

Breakfast	Lunch	Dinner
....	....	....
....	....	....
....	....	....
....	....	....
....	....	....
Snacks	....	....
....	....	....
....	....	....
....	....	....
....	....	....

6a   7   8   9   10   11   12p   1   2   3   4   5   6   7   8   9   10+

B=Breakfast   L=Lunch   D=Dinner   S=Snack   E=Exercise   M=Mind

Exercise ....

Mind ....

Emotional State

😃 ◯   🙂 ◯   😐 ◯   🙁 ◯

Contentment

0%   50%   100%

Sleep   Sleeping Time ....   # Times Wake Up at Night ....

Notes

....
....
....
....
....

Date .... Mo Tu We Th Fr Sa Su

Day (51)

Breakfast

....

....

....

....

....

Snacks

....

....

....

....

Lunch

....

....

....

....

....

....

....

....

....

Dinner

....

....

....

....

....

🕐 6a 7 8 9 10 11 12p 1 2 3 4 5 6 7 8 9 10+

B=Breakfast L=Lunch D=Dinner S=Snack E=Exercise M=Mind

Exercise ....

Mind ....

Emotional State

😀 ○ 🙂 ○ 😐 ○ ☹️ ○

Contentment

0%   50%   100%

Sleep   Sleeping Time ....   # Times Wake Up at Night ....

....

....

....

....

....

Notes

Day 52

Date .... Mo Tu We Th Fr Sa Su

Breakfast	Lunch	Dinner
....	....	....
....	....	....
....	....	....
....	....	....
....	....	....
Snacks	....	....
....	....	....
....	....	....
....	....	....
....	....	....

6a   7   8   9   10   11   12p   1   2   3   4   5   6   7   8   9   10+

B=Breakfast   L=Lunch   D=Dinner   S=Snack   E=Exercise   M=Mind

Exercise ....

Mind ....

Emotional State

😄 ○   🙂 ○   😐 ○   🙁 ○

Contentment

0%   50%   100%

Sleep   Sleeping Time ....   # Times Wake Up at Night ....

Notes   ....
....
....
....
....

Date .... Mo Tu We Th Fr Sa Su

Breakfast	Lunch	Dinner
....	....	....
....	....	....
....	....	....
....	....	....
....	....	....
Snacks	....	....
....	....	....
....	....	....
....	....	....
....	....	....

6a 7 8 9 10 11 12p 1 2 3 4 5 6 7 8 9 10+

B=Breakfast L=Lunch D=Dinner S=Snack E=Exercise M=Mind

Exercise ....

Mind ....

Emotional State   Contentment

😀 🙂 😐 🙁

0%   50%   100%

Sleep   Sleeping Time ....   # Times Wake Up at Night ....

....   **Notes**

....

....

....

....

Day

Date .... Mo Tu We Th Fr Sa Su

Breakfast	Lunch	Dinner
....	....	....
....	....	....
....	....	....
....	....	....
....	....	....
Snacks	....	....
....	....	....
....	....	....
....	....	....
....	....	....

6a 7 8 9 10 11 12p 1 2 3 4 5 6 7 8 9 10+

B=Breakfast L=Lunch D=Dinner S=Snack E=Exercise M=Mind

Exercise ....

Mind ....

Emotional State

😁 ○ 🙂 ○ 😐 ○ 🙁 ○

Contentment

0%   50%   100%

Sleep   Sleeping Time ....   # Times Wake Up at Night ....

Notes ....

....

....

....

....

Date .... Mo Tu We Th Fr Sa Su

Breakfast

....

....

....

....

....

Snacks

....

....

....

....

Lunch

....

....

....

....

....

....

....

....

....

....

Dinner

....

....

....

....

....

....

....

....

....

....

| 6a | 7 | 8 | 9 | 10 | 11 | 12p | 1 | 2 | 3 | 4 | 5 | 6 | 7 | 8 | 9 | 10+ |

B=Breakfast L=Lunch D=Dinner S=Snack E=Exercise M=Mind

Exercise ....

Mind ....

Emotional State

Contentment

0%   50%   100%

Sleep   Sleeping Time ....   # Times Wake Up at Night ....

Notes

....

....

....

....

....

Day 56

Date .... Mo Tu We Th Fr Sa Su

Breakfast

....

....

....

....

....

....

Snacks

....

....

....

....

Lunch

....

....

....

....

....

....

....

....

....

....

Dinner

....

....

....

....

....

....

....

....

....

6a 7 8 9 10 11 12p 1 2 3 4 5 6 7 8 9 10+

B=Breakfast L=Lunch D=Dinner S=Snack E=Exercise M=Mind

Exercise ....

Mind ....

Emotional State

○ ○ ○ ○

Contentment

0%   50%   100%

Sleep   Sleeping Time ....   # Times Wake Up at Night ....

Notes   ....

....

....

....

....

Date .... Mo Tu We Th Fr Sa Su

Breakfast

....
....
....
....
....

Snacks

....
....
....
....

Lunch

....
....
....
....
....
....
....
....
....
....

Dinner

....
....
....
....
....
....
....

6a 7 8 9 10 11 12p 1 2 3 4 5 6 7 8 9 10+

B=Breakfast L=Lunch D=Dinner S=Snack E=Exercise M=Mind

Exercise ....

Mind ....

Emotional State

Contentment

0%   50%   100%

Sleep   Sleeping Time ....   # Times Wake Up at Night ....

....   **Notes**
....
....
....
....

Day 58

Date ....   Mo Tu We Th Fr Sa Su

Breakfast

....

....

....

....

....

....

Snacks

....

....

....

....

Lunch

....

....

....

....

....

....

....

....

....

....

....

Dinner

....

....

....

....

....

....

....

....

6a 7 8 9 10 11 12p 1 2 3 4 5 6 7 8 9 10+

B=Breakfast L=Lunch D=Dinner S=Snack E=Exercise M=Mind

Exercise ....

Mind ....

Emotional State   **Contentment**

😀 🙂 😐 🙁

○   ○   ○   ○

0%   50%   100%

Sleep   Sleeping Time ....   # Times Wake Up at Night ....

Notes   ....

....

....

....

....

Date ....   Mo Tu We Th Fr Sa Su   Day (59)

Breakfast

....
....
....
....
....
....

Snacks

....
....
....
....

Lunch

....
....
....
....
....
....
....
....
....
....
....

Dinner

....
....
....
....
....
....
....
....
....
....
....

🕐   6a   7   8   9   10   11   12p   1   2   3   4   5   6   7   8   9   10+

B=Breakfast   L=Lunch   D=Dinner   S=Snack   E=Exercise   M=Mind

Exercise ....

Mind ....

Emotional State

😀 ☺ 😐 ☹
○ ○ ○ ○

Contentment

0%   50%   100%

Sleep   Sleeping Time ....   # Times Wake Up at Night ....

....
....
....
....
....

Notes

My Measurements

Arm ....

Hips ....

Calf ....

.... Chest

.... Waist

.... Belly

.... Thigh

Weight ....

BMI ....

Notes ....
....
....
....
....
....

Date .... Mo Tu We Th Fr Sa Su

Breakfast	Lunch	Dinner
....	....	....
....	....	....
....	....	....
....	....	....
....	....	....
Snacks	....	....
....	....	....
....	....	....
....	....	....
....	....	....

6a 7 8 9 10 11 12p 1 2 3 4 5 6 7 8 9 10+

B=Breakfast L=Lunch D=Dinner S=Snack E=Exercise M=Mind

Exercise ....

Mind ....

Emotional State   **Contentment**

0%   50%   100%

Sleep   Sleeping Time ....   # Times Wake Up at Night ....

....   **Notes**

....

....

....

....

Day

Date .... Mo Tu We Th Fr Sa Su

Breakfast

....

....

....

....

....

Snacks

....

....

....

....

Lunch

....

....

....

....

....

....

....

....

....

....

Dinner

....

....

....

....

....

....

....

6a 7 8 9 10 11 12p 1 2 3 4 5 6 7 8 9 10+

B=Breakfast L=Lunch D=Dinner S=Snack E=Exercise M=Mind

Exercise ....

Mind ....

Emotional State

○ ○ ○ ○

Contentment

0%   50%   100%

Sleep   Sleeping Time ....   # Times Wake Up at Night ....

Notes

....

....

....

....

....

Date .... Mo Tu We Th Fr Sa Su

Breakfast	Lunch	Dinner
....	....	....
....	....	....
....	....	....
....	....	....
....	....	....
	....	....
Snacks	....	....
....	....	....
....	....	....
....	....	....
....	....	....

6a   7   8   9   10   11   12p   1   2   3   4   5   6   7   8   9   10+

B=Breakfast   L=Lunch   D=Dinner   S=Snack   E=Exercise   M=Mind

Exercise ....

Mind ....

Emotional State

Contentment

0%   50%   100%

Sleep   Sleeping Time ....   # Times Wake Up at Night ....

Notes

....

....

....

....

....

Day

Date .... Mo Tu We Th Fr Sa Su

Breakfast	Lunch	Dinner
....	....	....
....	....	....
....	....	....
....	....	....
....	....	....
	....	....
Snacks	....	....
....	....	....
....	....	....
....	....	....
....	....	....

6a 7 8 9 10 11 12p 1 2 3 4 5 6 7 8 9 10+

B=Breakfast L=Lunch D=Dinner S=Snack E=Exercise M=Mind

Exercise ....

Mind ....

Emotional State   **Contentment**

○ ○ ○ ○   0%   50%   100%

Sleep   Sleeping Time ....   # Times Wake Up at Night ....

Notes ....
....
....
....
....

Date .... Mo Tu We Th Fr Sa Su

Breakfast

....
....
....
....
....
....

Snacks

....
....
....
....

Lunch

....
....
....
....
....
....
....
....
....
....
....
....

Dinner

....
....
....
....
....

| 6a | 7 | 8 | 9 | 10 | 11 | 12p | 1 | 2 | 3 | 4 | 5 | 6 | 7 | 8 | 9 | 10+ |

B=Breakfast L=Lunch D=Dinner S=Snack E=Exercise M=Mind

Exercise ....

Mind ....

Emotional State

Contentment

0%   50%   100%

Sleep   Sleeping Time ....   # Times Wake Up at Night ....

Notes

....
....
....
....
....

Day (65)

Date .... Mo Tu We Th Fr Sa Su

Breakfast

....

....

....

....

....

....

Snacks

....

....

....

....

Lunch

....

....

....

....

....

....

....

....

....

....

....

....

....

....

Dinner

....

....

....

....

....

....

....

....

....

6a 7 8 9 10 11 12p 1 2 3 4 5 6 7 8 9 10+

B=Breakfast L=Lunch D=Dinner S=Snack E=Exercise M=Mind

Exercise ....

Mind ....

Emotional State

Contentment

0%   50%   100%

Sleep   Sleeping Time ....   # Times Wake Up at Night ....

Notes

....

....

....

....

....

Date ....   Mo Tu We Th Fr Sa Su

Day (66)

Breakfast	Lunch	Dinner
....	....	....
....	....	....
....	....	....
....	....	....
....	....	....
Snacks	....	....
....	....	....
....	....	....
....	....	....
....	....	....

6a 7 8 9 10 11 12p 1 2 3 4 5 6 7 8 9 10+

B=Breakfast L=Lunch D=Dinner S=Snack E=Exercise M=Mind

Exercise ....

Mind ....

Emotional State

Contentment

0%   50%   100%

Sleep   Sleeping Time ....   # Times Wake Up at Night ....

....   **Notes**

....

....

....

....

Day

Date .... Mo Tu We Th Fr Sa Su

Breakfast	Lunch	Dinner
....	....	....
....	....	....
....	....	....
....	....	....
....	....	....
Snacks	....	....
....	....	....
....	....	....
....	....	....
....	....	....

6a 7 8 9 10 11 12p 1 2 3 4 5 6 7 8 9 10+

B=Breakfast L=Lunch D=Dinner S=Snack E=Exercise M=Mind

Exercise ....

Mind ....

Emotional State

Contentment

0%   50%   100%

Sleep   Sleeping Time ....   # Times Wake Up at Night ....

Notes   ....
....
....
....
....

Date ....   Mo   Tu   We   Th   Fr   Sa   Su

Breakfast	Lunch	Dinner
....	....	....
....	....	....
....	....	....
....	....	....
....	....	....
Snacks	....	....
....	....	....
....	....	....
....	....	....
....	....	....

6a   7   8   9   10   11   12p   1   2   3   4   5   6   7   8   9   10+

B=Breakfast   L=Lunch   D=Dinner   S=Snack   E=Exercise   M=Mind

Exercise ....

Mind ....

Emotional State

Contentment

0%   50%   100%

Sleep   Sleeping Time ....   # Times Wake Up at Night ....

....

....

....   **Notes**

....

....

Day

Date ....   Mo Tu We Th Fr Sa Su

Breakfast

....
....
....
....
....

Snacks

....
....
....
....

Lunch

....
....
....
....
....
....
....
....
....
....

Dinner

....
....
....
....
....
....
....
....
....

| 6a | 7 | 8 | 9 | 10 | 11 | 12p | 1 | 2 | 3 | 4 | 5 | 6 | 7 | 8 | 9 | 10+ |

B=Breakfast   L=Lunch   D=Dinner   S=Snack   E=Exercise   M=Mind

Exercise ....

Mind ....

Emotional State

😃 ○   🙂 ○   😐 ○   🙁 ○

Contentment

0%   50%   100%

Sleep   Sleeping Time ....   # Times Wake Up at Night ....

Notes
....
....
....
....
....

Date .... Mo Tu We Th Fr Sa Su

Day (70)

Breakfast	Lunch	Dinner
....	....	....
....	....	....
....	....	....
....	....	....
....	....	....
	....	....
Snacks	....	....
....	....	....
....	....	....
....	....	....
....	....	....

6a 7 8 9 10 11 12p 1 2 3 4 5 6 7 8 9 10+

B=Breakfast L=Lunch D=Dinner S=Snack E=Exercise M=Mind

Exercise ....

Mind ....

Emotional State

Contentment

0%   50%   100%

Sleep   Sleeping Time ....   # Times Wake Up at Night ....

....   Notes

....

....

....

....

Day

Date ....   Mo Tu We Th Fr Sa Su

Breakfast	Lunch	Dinner
....	....	....
....	....	....
....	....	....
....	....	....
....	....	....
....	....	....
Snacks	....	....
....	....	....
....	....	....
....	....	....
....	....	....

🕐   6a 7 8 9 10 11 12p 1 2 3 4 5 6 7 8 9 10+

B=Breakfast   L=Lunch   D=Dinner   S=Snack   E=Exercise   M=Mind

Exercise ....

Mind ....

Emotional State	Contentment
😃 ☺ 😐 🙁	0% 50% 100%
○ ○ ○ ○	

Sleep   Sleeping Time ....   # Times Wake Up at Night ....

Notes   ....

....

....

....

....

Date .... Mo Tu We Th Fr Sa Su

Breakfast	Lunch	Dinner
....	....	....
....	....	....
....	....	....
....	....	....
....	....	....
	....	....
Snacks	....	....
....	....	....
....	....	....
....	....	....
....	....	....

🕐 6a 7 8 9 10 11 12p 1 2 3 4 5 6 7 8 9 10+

B=Breakfast L=Lunch D=Dinner S=Snack E=Exercise M=Mind

Exercise ....

Mind ....

Emotional State

😀 ○   🙂 ○   😐 ○   🙁 ○

Contentment

0%   50%   100%

Sleep   Sleeping Time ....   # Times Wake Up at Night ....

.... Notes

....

....

....

....

Day 73

Date ....   Mo Tu We Th Fr Sa Su

Breakfast
....
....
....
....
....

Snacks
....
....
....
....

Lunch
....
....
....
....
....
....
....
....
....
....

Dinner
....
....
....
....
....
....
....
....

6a 7 8 9 10 11 12p 1 2 3 4 5 6 7 8 9 10+

B=Breakfast L=Lunch D=Dinner S=Snack E=Exercise M=Mind

Exercise ....

Mind ....

Emotional State

😃 🙂 😐 ☹️
○   ○   ○   ○

Contentment

0%   50%   100%

Sleep   Sleeping Time ....   # Times Wake Up at Night ....

Notes
....
....
....
....

Date .... Mo Tu We Th Fr Sa Su

Day (74)

Breakfast	Lunch	Dinner
....	....	....
....	....	....
....	....	....
....	....	....
....	....	....
Snacks	....	....
....	....	....
....	....	....
....	....	....
....	....	....

6a 7 8 9 10 11 12p 1 2 3 4 5 6 7 8 9 10+

B=Breakfast L=Lunch D=Dinner S=Snack E=Exercise M=Mind

Exercise ....

Mind ....

Emotional State

Contentment

0%   50%   100%

Sleep   Sleeping Time ....   # Times Wake Up at Night ....

....

....

....   **Notes**

....

....

....

Day (75)

Date .... Mo Tu We Th Fr Sa Su

Breakfast
....
....
....
....
....
....

Snacks
....
....
....
....

Lunch
....
....
....
....
....
....
....
....
....
....

Dinner
....
....
....
....
....
....

6a 7 8 9 10 11 12p 1 2 3 4 5 6 7 8 9 10+

B=Breakfast L=Lunch D=Dinner S=Snack E=Exercise M=Mind

Exercise ....

Mind ....

Emotional State
😃 ○ 🙂 ○ 😐 ○ 🙁 ○

Contentment
0%   50%   100%

Sleep   Sleeping Time ....   # Times Wake Up at Night ....

Notes ....
....
....
....

Date .... Mo Tu We Th Fr Sa Su

Breakfast	Lunch	Dinner
....	....	....
....	....	....
....	....	....
....	....	....
....	....	....
Snacks	....	....
....	....	....
....	....	....
....	....	....
....	....	....

6a 7 8 9 10 11 12p 1 2 3 4 5 6 7 8 9 10+

B=Breakfast L=Lunch D=Dinner S=Snack E=Exercise M=Mind

Exercise ....

Mind ....

Emotional State

Contentment

0%   50%   100%

Sleep   Sleeping Time ....   # Times Wake Up at Night ....

.... **Notes**

....

....

....

....

Day

Date ....

Mo Tu We Th Fr Sa Su

Breakfast	Lunch	Dinner
....	....	....
....	....	....
....	....	....
....	....	....
....	....	....
Snacks	....	....
....	....	....
....	....	....
....	....	....

6a   7   8   9   10   11   12p   1   2   3   4   5   6   7   8   9   10+

B=Breakfast   L=Lunch   D=Dinner   S=Snack   E=Exercise   M=Mind

Exercise ....

Mind ....

Emotional State

☺ ☺ 😐 ☹
○ ○ ○ ○

Contentment

0%   50%   100%

Sleep   Sleeping Time ....   # Times Wake Up at Night ....

Notes   ....
....
....
....
....

Date .... Mo Tu We Th Fr Sa Su   Day (78)

Breakfast | Lunch | Dinner
| | |
.... | .... | ....
.... | .... | ....
.... | .... | ....
.... | .... | ....
.... | .... | ....
| .... |
Snacks | .... |
| .... |
.... | .... | ....
.... | .... | ....
.... | .... | ....
.... | .... | ....

🕐 6a 7 8 9 10 11 12p 1 2 3 4 5 6 7 8 9 10+

B=Breakfast L=Lunch D=Dinner S=Snack E=Exercise M=Mind

Exercise ....

Mind ....

Emotional State   Contentment

😀 🙂 😐 🙁

○   ○   ○   ○   0%   50%   100%

Sleep   Sleeping Time ....   # Times Wake Up at Night ....

....   Notes
....
....
....
....

Day 79

Date .... Mo Tu We Th Fr Sa Su

Breakfast	Lunch	Dinner
....	....	....
....	....	....
....	....	....
....	....	....
....	....	....
Snacks	....	....
....	....	....
....	....	....
....	....	....
....	....	....

6a 7 8 9 10 11 12p 1 2 3 4 5 6 7 8 9 10+

B=Breakfast L=Lunch D=Dinner S=Snack E=Exercise M=Mind

Exercise ....

Mind ....

Emotional State   **Contentment**

😄 😊 😐 😟

0%   50%   100%

Sleep   Sleeping Time ....   # Times Wake Up at Night ....

Notes
....
....
....
....
....

Date ....   Mo Tu We Th Fr Sa Su

Breakfast	Lunch	Dinner
....	....	....
....	....	....
....	....	....
....	....	....
....	....	....
Snacks	....	....
....	....	....
....	....	....
....	....	....
....	....	....

6a   7   8   9   10   11   12p   1   2   3   4   5   6   7   8   9   10+

B=Breakfast L=Lunch D=Dinner S=Snack E=Exercise M=Mind

Exercise ....

Mind ....

Emotional State

Contentment

0%   50%   100%

Sleep   Sleeping Time ....   # Times Wake Up at Night ....

....

....

....   **Notes**

....

....

Day 81

Date ....   Mo Tu We Th Fr Sa Su

Breakfast	Lunch	Dinner
....	....	....
....	....	....
....	....	....
....	....	....
....	....	....
Snacks	....	....
....	....	....
....	....	....
....	....	....
....	....	....

6a 7 8 9 10 11 12p 1 2 3 4 5 6 7 8 9 10+

B=Breakfast L=Lunch D=Dinner S=Snack E=Exercise M=Mind

Exercise ....

Mind ....

Emotional State   Contentment

0%   50%   100%

Sleep   Sleeping Time ....   # Times Wake Up at Night ....

Notes

....

....

....

....

....

Date .... Mo Tu We Th Fr Sa Su

Breakfast	Lunch	Dinner
....	....	....
....	....	....
....	....	....
....	....	....
....	....	....
Snacks	....	....
....	....	....
....	....	....
....	....	....
....	....	....

🕐 6a 7 8 9 10 11 12p 1 2 3 4 5 6 7 8 9 10+

B=Breakfast   L=Lunch   D=Dinner   S=Snack   E=Exercise   M=Mind

Exercise ....

Mind ....

Emotional State
😀 ☺ 😐 ☹
○ ○ ○ ○

Contentment
0%   50%   100%

Sleep   Sleeping Time ....   # Times Wake Up at Night ....

....   **Notes**

....

....

....

....

Day 83

Date .... Mo Tu We Th Fr Sa Su

Breakfast
....
....
....
....
....
....

Snacks
....
....
....
....

Lunch
....
....
....
....
....
....
....
....
....
....

Dinner
....
....
....
....
....
....
....
....
....

6a 7 8 9 10 11 12p 1 2 3 4 5 6 7 8 9 10+

B=Breakfast L=Lunch D=Dinner S=Snack E=Exercise M=Mind

Exercise ....

Mind ....

Emotional State
😃 ◯ 🙂 ◯ 😐 ◯ 🙁 ◯

Contentment
0%   50%   100%

Sleep   Sleeping Time ....   # Times Wake Up at Night ....

Notes ....
....
....
....

Date .... Mo Tu We Th Fr Sa Su

Day (84)

Breakfast

....
....
....
....
....

Snacks

....
....
....
....

Lunch

....
....
....
....
....
....
....
....
....
....
....

Dinner

....
....
....
....
....
....
....
....
....
....
....

| 6a | 7 | 8 | 9 | 10 | 11 | 12p | 1 | 2 | 3 | 4 | 5 | 6 | 7 | 8 | 9 | 10+ |

B=Breakfast L=Lunch D=Dinner S=Snack E=Exercise M=Mind

Exercise ....

Mind ....

Emotional State

○ ○ ○ ○

Contentment

0%   50%   100%

Sleep   Sleeping Time .... # Times Wake Up at Night ....

.... Notes
....
....
....
....

Day (85)

Date ....   Mo Tu We Th Fr Sa Su

Breakfast

....
....
....
....
....
....

Snacks

....
....
....
....

Lunch

....
....
....
....
....
....
....
....
....
....
....

Dinner

....
....
....
....
....
....

6a 7 8 9 10 11 12p 1 2 3 4 5 6 7 8 9 10+

B=Breakfast L=Lunch D=Dinner S=Snack E=Exercise M=Mind

Exercise ....

Mind ....

Emotional State

○ ○ ○ ○

Contentment

0%   50%   100%

Sleep   Sleeping Time ....   # Times Wake Up at Night ....

Notes   ....
....
....
....
....

Date .... Mo Tu We Th Fr Sa Su

Day (86)

Breakfast	Lunch	Dinner
....	....	....
....	....	....
....	....	....
....	....	....
....	....	....
	....	....
Snacks	....	....
....	....	....
....	....	....
....	....	....
....	....	....

🕐 6a 7 8 9 10 11 12p 1 2 3 4 5 6 7 8 9 10+

B=Breakfast L=Lunch D=Dinner S=Snack E=Exercise M=Mind

Exercise ....

Mind ....

Emotional State

😀 ⃝ 🙂 ⃝ 😐 ⃝ 🙁 ⃝

Contentment

0%   50%   100%

Sleep   Sleeping Time ....   # Times Wake Up at Night ....

.... Notes

....

....

....

....

Day Date .... Mo Tu We Th Fr Sa Su

Breakfast

....
....
....
....
....
....

Snacks

....
....
....
....

Lunch

....
....
....
....
....
....
....
....
....
....
....
....

Dinner

....
....
....
....
....
....
....
....

6a   7   8   9   10   11   12p   1   2   3   4   5   6   7   8   9   10+
B=Breakfast   L=Lunch   D=Dinner   S=Snack   E=Exercise   M=Mind

Exercise ....

Mind ....

Emotional State

○ ○ ○ ○

Contentment

0%   50%   100%

Sleep   Sleeping Time ....   # Times Wake Up at Night ....

Notes

....
....
....
....
....

Date .... Mo Tu We Th Fr Sa Su

Day 88

Breakfast

....
....
....
....
....

Snacks

....
....
....
....

Lunch

....
....
....
....
....
....
....
....
....
....

Dinner

....
....
....
....
....

6a 7 8 9 10 11 12p 1 2 3 4 5 6 7 8 9 10+

B=Breakfast L=Lunch D=Dinner S=Snack E=Exercise M=Mind

Exercise ....

Mind ....

Emotional State

Contentment

0%   50%   100%

Sleep   Sleeping Time ....   # Times Wake Up at Night ....

....
....
....
....
....

Notes

Day (89)

Date .... Mo Tu We Th Fr Sa Su

Breakfast
....
....
....
....
....

Snacks
....
....
....
....

Lunch
....
....
....
....
....
....
....
....
....
....
....

Dinner
....
....
....
....
....

| 6a | 7 | 8 | 9 | 10 | 11 | 12p | 1 | 2 | 3 | 4 | 5 | 6 | 7 | 8 | 9 | 10+ |

B=Breakfast L=Lunch D=Dinner S=Snack E=Exercise M=Mind

Exercise ....

Mind ....

Emotional State
○ ○ ○ ○

Contentment
0%   50%   100%

Sleep   Sleeping Time ....   # Times Wake Up at Night ....

Notes
....
....
....
....
....

Date ....   Mo Tu We Th Fr Sa Su   Day (90)

Breakfast

....
....
....
....
....
....

Snacks

....
....
....
....

Lunch

....
....
....
....
....
....
....
....
....
....
....

Dinner

....
....
....
....
....
....
....
....

🕐 6a 7 8 9 10 11 12p 1 2 3 4 5 6 7 8 9 10+

B=Breakfast L=Lunch D=Dinner S=Snack E=Exercise M=Mind

Exercise ....

Mind ....

Emotional State

😀 ○   🙂 ○   😐 ○   ☹️ ○

Contentment

0%   50%   100%

Sleep   Sleeping Time ....   # Times Wake Up at Night ....

....   **Notes**
....
....
....
....

HIP HIP HURRAY!

Day **90**

My Measurements

Arm ....

Hips ....

Calf ....

.... Chest

.... Waist

.... Belly

.... Thigh

Weight ....

BMI ....

Conclusion ....
....
....
....
....
....

Notes

MY RESULTS

Day (1)
BEFORE

Chest ....

Arm ....

Waist ....

Belly ....

Hips ....

Thigh ....

Calf ....

Weight ....

BMI ....

Day (90)
AFTER

.... Chest

.... Arm

.... Waist

.... Belly

.... Hips

.... Thigh

.... Calf

.... Weight

.... BMI

Copyright © Cute Food Diary Ideas
"My 90 Days Diet Journal" Published by: Studio 5519, 1732 1st Ave #25519 New York, NY 10128
January 2017, Issue no. 1 (Version 1.1); Contact: info@studio5519.com; Date: January 31st 2017; illustration credits: © StockUnlimited

26927389R00060

Printed in Great Britain
by Amazon